AF449064

Sophia's Sunstar
By Laurie Mandel
Illustrated By Mehtab Jamil

Sophia's Sunstar

"A STORY BOOK FOR CHILDREN"

Written by: Laurie Mandel
in8wisdom@gmail.com
Illustrations by: Mehtab Jamil

Dedication

To my niece Lyndsie on your 6th birthday~

This is for you and all children who are discovering
the courage, curiosity, and comfort
of their own inner Sunstar.
May you know this magical inner light
is always inside of you.

♥

Everyday when she wakes up, Sophia goes to her window next to her bed. Sophia LOVES the sunshine!

1

She knows that the sun loves the flowers because
they grow after a rainfall.
She knows the sun loves spiders because it makes
their web shine.

4

And Sophia really knows that the sun loves her
because it makes her belly feel warm and loved inside.
The sun is her special friend. She calls it her "Sunstar."

Sometimes even when Sophia feels mad, sad, or scared, she seems to feel a little better because she knows she always has Sunstar with her. Sophia says Sunstar is a calmness she feels inside her belly.

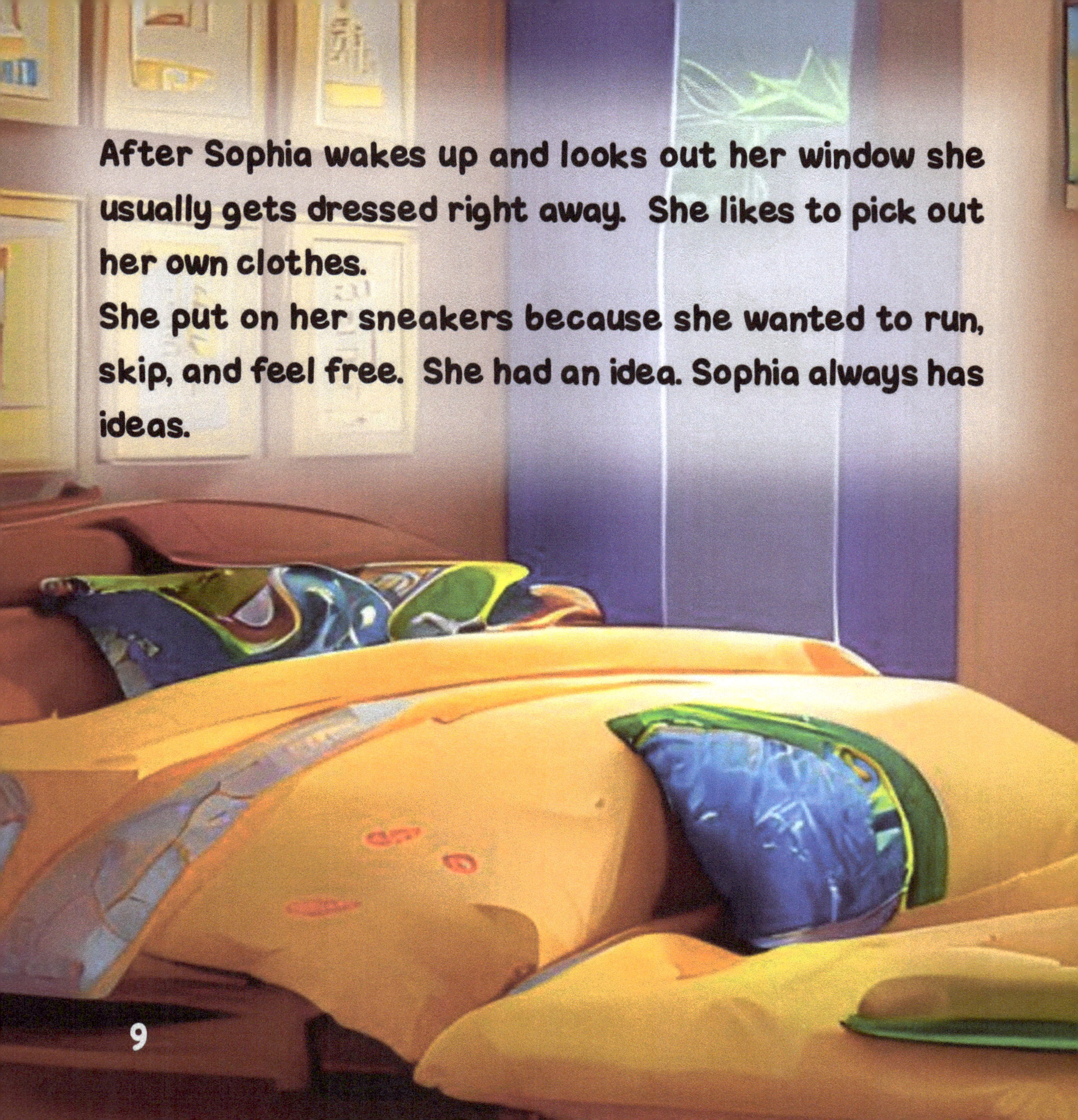

After Sophia wakes up and looks out her window she usually gets dressed right away. She likes to pick out her own clothes.
She put on her sneakers because she wanted to run, skip, and feel free. She had an idea. Sophia always has ideas.

9

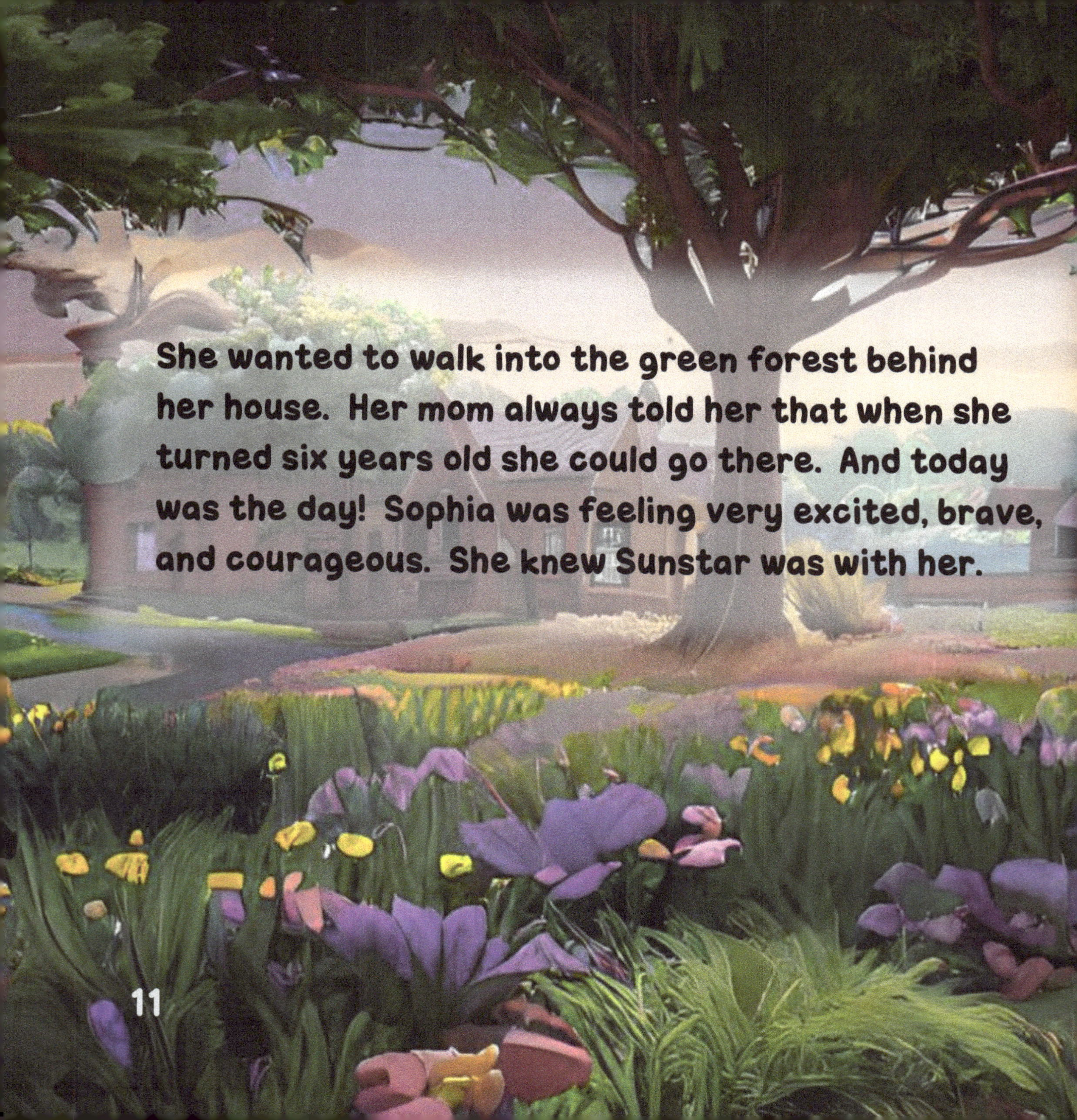

She wanted to walk into the green forest behind her house. Her mom always told her that when she turned six years old she could go there. And today was the day! Sophia was feeling very excited, brave, and courageous. She knew Sunstar was with her.

The green trees were so tall.
The blue-green stream was so calm.
The orange and purple flowers were so bright.
The air felt so warm.
Everything looked and felt so magical!

13

Out of the corner of her eye, she caught a glimpse of something amazing. Something unbelievable!!

15

It was the most beautiful...
16

....b u t t e r f l y!

Its wings were not like anything Sophia has ever seen before. The colors were magnificent! They were purple, blue, orange, yellow, and pink!

Before she could even blink, the beautiful butterfly scooped her up onto its wings.

17

"Faster! Faster! I'm flying!" Sophia shouted as she giggled.
18

Sophia's eyes were wide open. She had the biggest smile on her face.

She saw the tops of the big trees, the flowers, and the stream from so high above.

19

20

Then, Sophia took a peek behind her. What did she see?
A dark rain cloud. It began to rain. Sophia was getting
all wet. And started to feel scared. She thought for a
moment and remembered what to do.

She closed her eyes and said:

"Sunstar, Sunstar
I'm a bit afraid you see,
Please wrap your sunrays
All around me."

24

She opened her eyes and what do you know? The
butterfly gently lowered Sophia down onto the petals
of a huge yellow sunflower -- right in her own
backyard.
25

That night before Sophia went to sleep, she told her mom all about her day. "It was beautiful, mom! I was flying on the wings of this most beautiful, butterfly! When it started to rain, I didn't like that very much. But I talked to Sunstar and I wasn't so afraid anymore."

27

I closed my eyes and said:
"Sunstar, Sunstar
I'm a bit afraid you see,
Please wrap your sun rays
All around me."

28

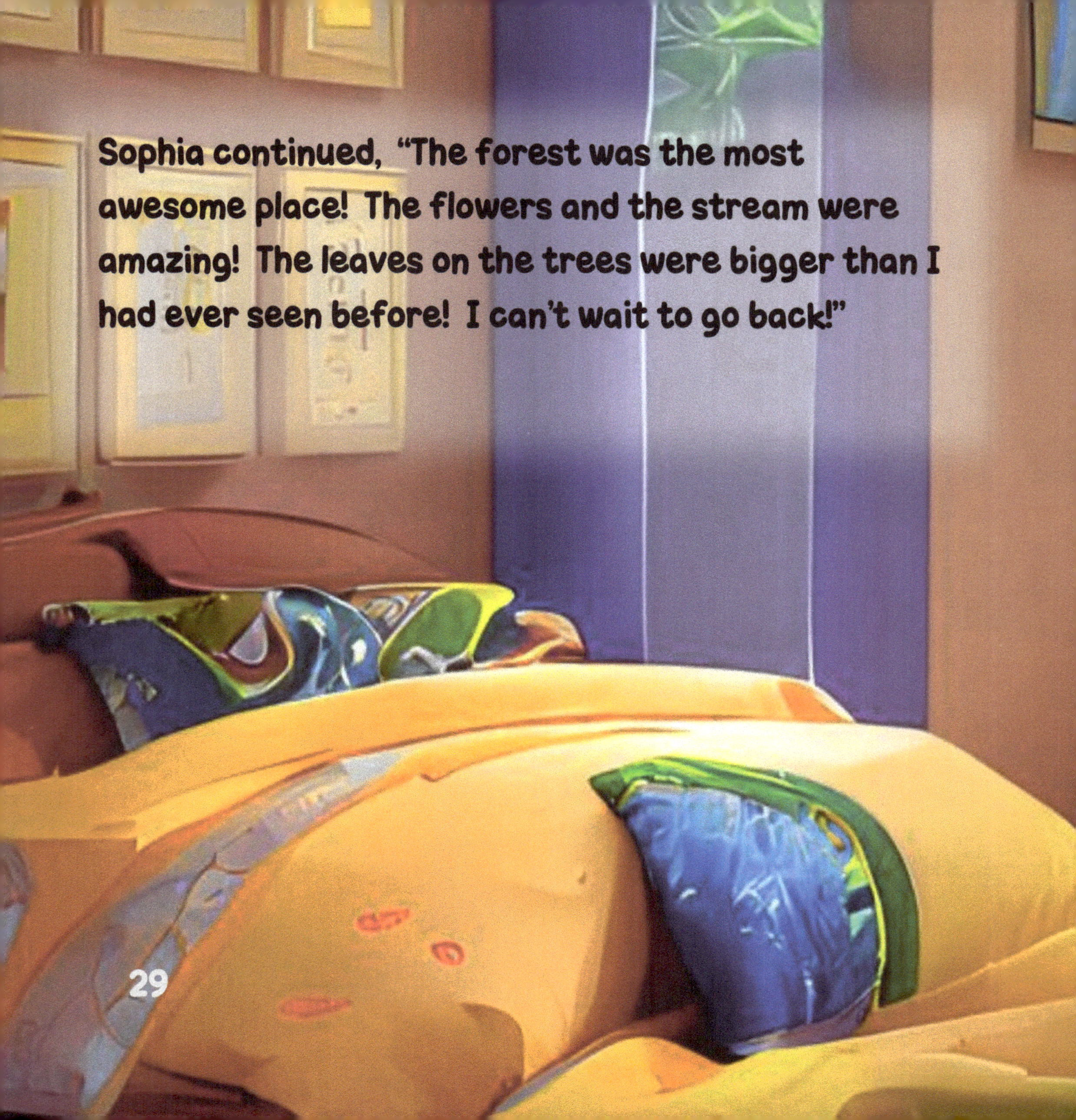

Sophia continued, "The forest was the most awesome place! The flowers and the stream were amazing! The leaves on the trees were bigger than I had ever seen before! I can't wait to go back!"

29

Her mom replied, "Sophia, that is wonderful! I'm so proud
of you! What a great experience. You are so brave."

And what made Sophia's day even more special was feeling
Sunstar inside her belly -- a feeling which made her
feel courageous, calm, and confident inside.

About the Author

Laurie Mandel is creative, artsy, and a true explorer at heart. Growing up on Long Island, Laurie was fascinated with the incredible beauty of nature and the magic of butterflies.

A former art teacher, Laurie dedicated her career to inspiring youth to explore their inner artist as well as to find their voice to navigate the slippery slope of social relationships in school.

"Sophia's Sunstar" is Laurie's first children's book. As a child, when she felt anxious, Laurie believed that the sun shined inside her like a superpower, which helped her feel strong. She hopes this book will help other children discover their inner strength and what truly lights them up. Laurie loves photography, painting, yoga, swimming, dancing, astrology, kindness, and growing amazing zinnia gardens.

www.ingramcontent.com/pod-product-compliance
Lightning Source LLC
Chambersburg PA
CBHW041952130726
48010CB00022B/141